TWO HUNDRED YEARS OF BICYCLES

Jim Murphy

J.B. Lippincott
New York

For Scooby-doo—sometimes known as Teresa Murphy

Acknowledgments

It would be impossible to gather all the information and photographs for a project of this sort without the help of others. The author would like to thank the following individuals and organizations for their valuable and generous assistance: Don H. Berkebile, Associate Curator, Division of Transportation, Smithsonian Institution; Susan E. Hecklau of Cycles Peugeot; Peter Boor, International Human-Powered Vehicle Association; Sidney Star of Alpha Cycle and Supply Corp.; Tim Downing, Kirtland/Tourpak; Cathy Butsko of the Museum of the City of New York; Stephen Morikawa, American Honda Motor Co.; Dolores Nash, *Bicycling* magazine; Walter Ezell, *American Wheelmen* magazine; GemPhoto, Inc.; Motobecane America; Matsuri; Nichibei Fuji Cycle Company; Kabuki Bicycle; Trek Bicycles; Tom Cogan; Lois Krieger; Philip Menninger; and Al Kreitler.

Photo credits: Alpha Cycle and Supply Corporation, 47, 49, 50; American Honda Motor Company, Incorporated, 16; *Bicycling Magazine*, iv, 53, 55; Cycles Peugeot, USA, 31, 32, 34, 37, 41, 47, 48, 56, 57; GemPhoto, 1, 2, 3, 5, 6, 7, 8, 11, 24, 27, 33; *The History of the Velocipede*, 4; Kirtland / Tourpak, 51; Joe Martin/Philip B. Menninger, 51; Jim Murphy, 51; Museum of the City of New York, 10, 14, 17, 25, 26, 27, 37, 39; Yiorgos Naoum, 52; Smithsonian Institution, 9, 12, 13, 15, 16, 18, 20, 21, 23, 24, 29, 30, 31, 33, 36, 40, 42, 43, 45; U.S. Bureau of Public Roads, 28; U.S. Patent Office, 27.

Two Hundred Years of Bicycles
Copyright © 1983 by Jim Murphy
All rights reserved. Printed in the United States of America.

Library of Congress Cataloging in Publication Data
Murphy, Jim, 1947-
   Two hundred years of bicycles.
   Summary: Traces the history of bicycles from the French "celerifere" of 1791, through the nineteenth-century velocipede, hobby horse, boneshaker, and high-wheeler, to the modern racing bicycle and HPV.
   1. Bicycles—History—Juvenile literature.
[1. Bicycles and bicycling—History]   I. Title.
TL400.M87 1983   629.2′272   81-48608
ISBN 0-397-32007-8
ISBN 0-398-32008-6 (lib. bdg.)

1 2 3 4 5 6 7 8 9 10
First Edition

Contents

Acknowledgments   ii

Introduction   1

1. "Fast Feet"   3

2. The Boneshaker   10

3. The Ordinary   17

4. The Tricycle   30

5. From Safety to Modern Racer   35

6. Human-Powered Vehicles   52

Anatomy of a Bicycle   56

For Further Reading   58

Index   59

Introduction

Look up just about any busy street and you'll probably see someone riding a bicycle. That's because there are over 100 million bicycles in the United States! And 7 million new ones will be bought this year alone.

When we talk about bicycles, most of us think of sleek, ten- or twelve-speed machines with skinny wheels and turned-down handlebars. But bicycles have been around for a very long time and have come in a lot of different sizes and shapes.

Bicycle historians don't know who first had the idea to use human power to move two- and three-wheeled vehicles. No really old bicycles or tricycles have ever been found. And the drawings and written records that do exist are very unclear.

It is believed that the Egyptians had bicycles over 3000 years ago. Historians think they can see bicyclelike machines in drawings found in some tombs. Since the Egyptians did make lightweight wooden wheels with spokes and were clever builders, it is possible that a carpenter connected two wheels to a wooden frame and rolled off along the Nile.

The bicycle did not make its next appearance until 1490. In that year the great artist and inventor Leonardo da Vinci made this doodle at the bottom of a notebook page. The drawing shows a three-wheeled vehicle that looks a lot like a tricycle. Leonardo may have meant this to carry a small cannon as well as the soldier to fire it.

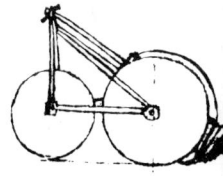

Da Vinci's tricycle

Three years later, Leonardo did another bicycle sketch. This one shows a two-wheeler and appears to be moved by a pedal-chain device. Unfortunately, Leonardo never developed his tricycle or bicycle beyond his rough drawings.

After this a few history books mention "races on wheeled horses." But there are no descriptions of what these machines looked like or how they worked. In 1642, however, there is another hint that bicycles may have been made. That was when a craftsman designed a window for a church at Stokes Poges, England. The window shows a young boy sitting on an uncomfortable, wooden saddle mounted on wheels. The window maker may have been showing a popular children's toy of the time.

Stokes Poges two-wheeler

These references aren't very helpful for learning about ancient bicycles. In fact, we're not sure that any of these two- or three-wheeled vehicles were ever built.

This book describes the first bicycles we're sure existed and tells how they were changed and improved over the past 200 years. It shows how people have used bicycles in their work and play—and lets you see the bicycles we'll be riding in the future.

[2]

1 "Fast Feet"

On a summer day in 1791, the giant lawn of Louis XVI's royal palace was crowded with ladies and gentlemen. Some were playing croquet. Others watched the game or strolled peacefully along the flower-lined paths. Suddenly, there was a clatter and then a loud squeaking. The next instant, the people saw the Comte de Sivrac running madly through the middle of the croquet field.

Celerifere in action

But de Sivrac wasn't really running. His feet were pushing along the ground in a running motion, but he was sitting on a strange "wooden horse" with wheels. When de Sivrac reached the end of the lawn, he turned his machine around and came zooming back.

De Sivrac's "hobbyhorse" was a simple, wooden frame mounted on two wooden wheels. For balance, there was a handle on the frame. The machine wasn't very big. De Sivrac sat only about thirty inches above the ground.

The hobbyhorse takes on a real horse

The hobbyhorse became an instant hit with rich, young men of Louis's court. Soon they were racing each other along the streets of Paris and across open fields. There are even reports that some raced against horses. After a while, the machine was given a name. It was called a celerifere, which means "swift footed" in French.

The celerifere required very strong legs to get up hills. And since it didn't have brakes, going downhill could be a wild and dangerous ride. But the celerifere's biggest drawback was that it couldn't be steered. It only went in a straight line. If a rider wanted to turn, he had to stop and point it the way he wanted to go. Skilled riders made turns by lifting the front wheel while in motion and pulling it in the right direction. Without knowing it, these riders were doing the world's first wheelies.

It took another twenty-six years before a German baron, Karl von Drais, came up with a way to steer a celerifere. Von Drais was the chief forester for the grand duke of Baden, Austria, and he often used a celerifere to patrol the woodlands. But the forest paths he traveled were full of twists and turns. Von Drais had to lift and drag his celerifere so much that each patrol left him tired and sweaty.

To solve the problem, von Drais attached a triangular, wooden frame to each side of the front wheel. Then he bolted this to the main frame. A wooden rudder let von Drais turn the front wheel to the left or right. Not only could he follow the winding trails, but he could avoid rocks and bumps, too. A few years after this, von Drais added a padded seat and an armrest.

The Draisienne

The armrest had two uses. While rolling down steep hills a rider leaned against it for balance. Leaning against the armrest also let the rider push harder against the ground and go faster. Von Drais claimed that his machine could go nine miles per hour on a dry, flat road. Downhill, he said it was as fast as a galloping horse.

Von Drais named his invention after himself. He called it the Draisienne. Soon he became a celebrity and traveled all over Europe to demonstrate his machine.

As its popularity spread, it was sometimes given other names. In England, it was called the Dandy Horse, the Pedestrian Hobby Horse, and the Swiftwalker. In France, the old celerifere's name was changed slightly to velocipede, which means "fast feet." Eventually, velocipede became the most common name for von Drais's machine.

During the next twenty years, only a few changes were made

An English gentleman demonstrating his velocipede

in the velocipede. The illustration shows a finely dressed English gentleman, complete with top hat, riding an 1827 model. The wheels are a little larger than the ones on either de Sivrac's or von Drais's machines. And the saddle is bigger and fancier. Both changes raised the rider higher off the ground and made running, turning, and stopping difficult.

To help people master velocipede riding, special schools were set up. One such school was Johnson's Pedestrian Hobby Horse School, located in London. Riders circled a small, dirt track hundreds of times, while the watchful instructor called out directions to them. The illustration also shows another improvement in the velocipede. The front and rear wheels are no longer held to the frame by wood. Instead, two metal prongs, called forks, do the job. Metal forks were heavier, but they didn't crack like wood if the rider hit a sharp bump.

Usually, only men rode velocipedes. The long dresses that were fashionable back then made it impossible for a woman to hop

Johnson's Pedestrian Hobby Horse School

aboard and run along. In addition, many people felt that velocipede riding wasn't dignified. So that women wouldn't be left behind, three-wheeled vehicles were created. Most people didn't realize it then, but these three-wheelers were a major improvement over the velocipede. They were the first machines designed so the rider did not have to push along the ground in order to move.

This 1819 Ladies' Hobby Horse is an example of an early three-wheeler. It was powered by floor paddles and handgrips. Metal rods and rope go from the paddles and handgrips to a crank on the front wheel. When the rider pumped the paddles and pulled on the handgrips, the rope turned the crank and made the Hobby Horse move forward. A small handle on the metal frame was used for steering.

The Ladies' Hobby Horse wasn't easy to ride. The machine weighed almost 200 pounds, which made working the paddles

The Ladies' Hobby Horse

and handgrips very tiring. And if a rider came to a steep hill, she had to climb out and push.

The Ladies' Hobby Horse may not have worked very well, but velocipede makers were intrigued by it. They liked the way the hands and feet combined to move the machine and tried to use the idea on a two-wheeler. Lewis Gompertz, of Surrey, England, created one of the best ones in 1821.

Gompertz put a curved bar with teeth at the base of the steering handle. He also put a small, toothed circle of wood, called a pinion, at the center of the wheel. When the handle was pulled back, the curved, toothed bar turned the pinion and the wheel. After each pull, the turning of the wheel pushed the pinion inward automatically. This allowed the handle to be returned to the forward position.

The Gompertz velocipede

Just imagine a Gompertz velocipede in action. The rider's arms are pumping the handle back and forth furiously and his legs are running along the ground. It must have been a very funny sight to see one coming up the road. Still, it had advantages over the most popular form of transportation back then, the horse. It didn't need a special stable area, grooming, or food. And it must have worked pretty well, too. In the 1830s, a number of French towns bought the machine to speed up the delivery of their mail.

2 The Boneshaker

Pierre Michaux pushed open the door to his carriage shop and wheeled his velocipede out. A moment later, he was sailing down the Boulevard Saint-Martin in Paris—and everyone was staring at him. Michaux's feet never touched the ground!

After the improvements made by Gompertz, no major changes were made in the velocipede during the next forty years. Most people got so tired of pushing around the heavy two-wheelers that they either threw them away or broke them up for firewood. Then, in 1863, Michaux had a very bright idea. He added a set of metal pedals to the front wheel.

A gentleman on his boneshaker

Michaux never left any record of how he got the idea for pedals. It's possible that it came to him after he studied the way a hand-operated grindstone worked. The wheel of the grindstone was made to go around by a handle connected directly to the stone. Michaux may have realized that the same prin-

[10]

ciple could be used to turn the wheel of a velocipede, only using both feet.

The pedal-driven velocipede allowed riders to sit tall on the seat and calmly pedal down any road. When the machine went downhill, the pedals continued to turn, so riders took their feet off the pedals and dangled them to the side. A few models came with footrests on a metal bar above the front wheel. This allowed the rider to put his feet up comfortably and just sail along.

A wobbly boneshaker ride

Michaux and one of his assistants, Pierre Lallement, made another improvement in the velocipede. They changed the steering device. Instead of the von Drais rudder, they had handlebars that the rider held with both hands. Two-handed steering gave the rider better control when turning.

The photograph shows an expensive, pedal-driven velocipede that was built in 1868. The frame and tires are made of solid iron, with the fittings made of brass. Instead of simply attaching the seat to the hard frame, the builders mounted it on a rigid steel

The 1868 boneshaker

spring. It's possible that they saw how coach springs helped cushion the ride over a bumpy road and hoped it would do the same for the velocipede rider.

All pedal-driven velocipedes were built with a slightly larger front wheel. That's because each turn of the pedal only made the wheel go around one time. So the bigger the front wheel, the farther the velocipede would go with each turn. The front wheel of this velocipede is 37 inches tall. That meant that with each turn of the wheel it traveled over 116 inches.

Another new feature of the pedal-driven velocipede was a brake. The 1868 model has a cord running from the right handgrip to a pad, called a brake shoe, near the rear wheel. When the rider twisted the handgrip, the cord pulled at the brake shoe and made it rub against the tire. This really didn't stop a speeding machine, but it did slow it down a little.

Even with the improvements, the pedal-driven velocipede wasn't easy to ride. Many models weighed over 100 pounds. A long trip was a tiring chore even for the hardiest rider.

To make things worse, the metal tires and frame and the hard seat made hitting even a small bump a teeth-rattling, bone-jarring experience. After a while, the word velocipede was replaced by another more accurate name—the boneshaker!

Once again, schools had to be set up to teach proper hand and foot coordination. The illustration shows a very clumsy group of men struggling to stay aboard their boneshakers.

A New York boneshaker school

Whatever the problems, people seemed to like the boneshaker. By 1865, Pierre Michaux's carriage shop was turning out 400 of them a year. Ten years later, New York City boasted of having over 5000 boneshakers on the road.

As interest in the boneshaker increased, inventors began fiddling with the design. One variation was the two-seater, or tandem.

The builder simply added a seat above the rear wheel and another set of pedals. The extra pedals came in handy when the second rider was a man. But women still wore long dresses and usually rode side-saddle. This left all of the work to the rider in front.

Boneshaker tandem

Probably the most amazing variation of the boneshaker was made around 1869 by an American named Sylvester Roper.

Roper developed a small steam engine and fitted it between the wheels of a wooden velocipede. The boiler had two parts. The bottom held a hot charcoal fire to heat the water. The top was where the water was boiled and turned to steam. Rising steam was fed through metal tubes to two cylinders located on either side of the chimney. The pressure of the steam made rods inside the cylinders move back and forth, which turned the rear wheel. Extra water was held under the long seat, while smoke from the fire escaped through the chimney.

Roper's machine worked so well that people paid twenty-five

cents just to see him race horses or ride it up hills. But his steam velocipede was never manufactured for sale. Early steam engines made a lot of hissing and chugging noise. And if the rider didn't check the water level and fire carefully, the entire engine could blow up.

Roper steam velocipede

Toward the end of the nineteenth century, however, when reliable gasoline engines were designed, people once again thought about putting motors on bicycles. This Indian Motorcycle was designed and built by a famous bicycle racer, Oscar Hedstrom, in 1902. He simply attached a small gas engine to a standard bicycle and puttered down the street. Notice that Hedstrom left the pedals on his machine. If he had engine problems, he could pedal home and make the repairs.

Indian motorcycle   Honda XR500R

    Since then motorcycles have been made more powerful. And special tires and shock absorbers have been added. The entire shape of the motorcycle has changed so much it's hard to see that the basic shape is that of a bicycle. Even so, the next time you see a motorcycle like the Honda XR500R streaking along a dusty trail, remember that Sylvester Roper started it all, over 100 years ago.

3 The Ordinary

At exactly eight o'clock in the morning, the bugler sounded the call. Instantly, the forty members of the riding club jumped onto their steeds and rode out of the park in perfect formation.

They weren't soldiers. And they weren't riding horses, either. They were members of the Brooklyn-based Germantown Bicycle Club and they were riding the high-wheeler—a machine that was

The Germantown Bicycle Club sets off

such a common sight at the end of the nineteenth century that it was known as the "ordinary."

How did the boneshaker turn into this strange-looking bicycle?

The boneshaker's biggest problem was its weight. A 100-pound boneshaker made it impossible to go very far or very fast. So designers looked for ways to make the machine lighter.

They replaced the solid iron frame with one made of hollow metal tubes. Next, instead of solid iron tires, rubber tires were cemented onto light, metal rims. And the heavy, wooden spokes began to be made of thin wire. No one knows who thought up these changes or exactly when. We do know that they were all demonstrated at the first cycle show held in 1869 at Pre-Catalan, France.

After this, designers enlarged the front wheel. The reason for this is very simple. A 37-inch wheel allowed the boneshaker to travel 116 inches with one turn of the pedal. A 60-inch wheel lets the ordinary travel 188 inches. That's over 15 feet!

The earliest high-wheelers appeared at the Pre-Catalan cycle show in 1869. Again, we don't really know who made the first

The standard Columbia ordinary

one. Two years later James Starley, of Coventry, England, introduced an ordinary that he called the Ariel. The Ariel was extremely light and became so popular that Starley was soon called "the father of the cycle industry."

Surprisingly, the ordinary was much lighter than the boneshaker. Most weighed between fifty and sixty pounds. A few racing models weighed under twenty-five pounds.

The ordinary had its problems, however. For instance, getting on the seat took a great deal of skill.

Each ordinary had a tiny, metal step on the frame just above the rear wheel. The rider put one foot on the step and, while holding the handlebars, pushed along the ground with the other foot. Once he was moving fast, the rider would jump up and onto the seat.

New riders often had to be helped up by a friend or had to use a ladder. And many of them ended up in a ditch instead of gliding smoothly down the street.

Probably the most dangerous part of riding an ordinary was stopping. The rider sat directly above the pedals. If he put the brake on too hard, the front wheel would stop, but there was a good chance the rider would be pitched over the handlebars and land on his head. Since the head of the rider was almost eight feet in the air, doing a "header" could cause serious injury. There are even reports of deaths due to falling from a high-wheeler.

Whatever the dangers, there were over 30,000 ordinaries in the United States by 1880. Several factors added to the popularity of this unusual machine.

First, bicycle riding clubs began to be formed. The earliest in America was the Boston Bicycle Club, founded in 1878. Here twenty-nine of its members are about to depart on a tour of the Massachusetts countryside.

This and most other clubs followed the rules of the army cavalry. A few members were selected as officers. They decided

The Boston Bicycle Club

where the club would travel to and what routes would be taken. They also signaled for various riding formations. The group usually rode two-by-two on an empty back road. When going through a town, they would ride single file. A bugler led the club and warned people of their approach by blowing his horn.

During the next twenty years, bicycle clubs were formed in hundreds of towns throughout the United States. These local clubs joined with the national bicycle club, called the League of American Wheelmen, to get highways and streets improved for smoother riding. Most clubs had simpler goals. They wanted to teach people how to ride the big machines without hurting themselves or others.

A few clubs did have special membership requirements. To get into the Rising Sun Cycle Club a rider had to be Japanese. There was even a Fat Man's Cycle Club in Brooklyn, New York. Membership was limited to riders who weighed over 250 pounds!

The second factor in the growing popularity of the ordinary was bicycle racing. At first, races were organized by the local riding clubs and attended by only a few townspeople. This all changed when an American bicycle racer, Will Pitman, made headline news in the summer of 1878.

Pitman pedaled to victory in a one-mile race in three minutes and fifty-five seconds. Modern runners can cover a mile quicker than that, but in 1878 Pitman's time was an amazing feat. After his victory, more and more people came to watch the speedy ordinaries compete. Special tracks had to be built and racers were payed according to how they finished in a race.

Here the English racer M. W. Wright stands beside his bicycle. Notice that Wright's pants and shirt are skin-tight and that the arms of his shirt have been cut off. This allowed the air he was riding through to slide easily around his body. And he didn't want a flapping pant leg to get caught in the wheel and send him crashing to the ground.

Wright's bicycle looks like any other ordinary, but there are

M. W. Wright beside his racer

some differences. For one thing, it was very light. This ordinary weighed just under thirty pounds. Also, the back of the seat is turned up sharply. This let Wright pedal as hard as possible without slipping off accidentally. The tool kit that was usually attached to the back of the seat had been removed, too. Wright's bicycle has a brake in this photo. But before each race, he removed it to make his bicycle lighter. If he had to stop for any reason, all that Wright could do was take his feet off the pedals and slow his machine until he could safely leap to the ground.

[23]

Races were usually from one to twenty-five miles in length. A few covered several hundred miles. The riders would mount their ordinaries and line up at the start, while an assistant held them up. When the starter fired the gun, the assistant would push his rider forward.

The race is about to begin

The riders shot away from the start, pedaling as hard as they could. For a one-mile race, they would go at full speed for the entire distance. No racer could pedal this hard for the longer races. So once around the first turn, the riders would slow down a little to conserve energy.

Racers go into the first turn

During a race, many riders might take the lead. And faster riders were always passing the slower ones. To make sure no rider committed a foul by cutting another off, spotters stood at different parts of the track. This drawing is of a twenty-five-mile race held at the American Institute in New York City. The two men in the infield are the spotters. Spotters had another job, too. If there was an accident, they were supposed to pull the injured riders off the track before someone ran over them.

Race at the American Institute

Bicycle clubs and racing kept the ordinary in the news and kept people going to the store. Sales rose to over 9000 bicycles a year after 1880. But even though it was popular, designers began altering the basic shape. Some were hoping to make the ordinary safer, while others attempted to make it more useful—and increase sales while they were at it.

For instance, after 1882, bicycles appeared that had the smaller wheel in front and the larger wheel in the rear. This design appealed to timid riders because it lessened the chance of a "header." But the position of the pedals made pedaling awkward, so most people stayed with the big front wheel.

Ordinaries with small front wheels

Some manufacturers made a smaller version of the ordinary for children. Others introduced an ordinary, called the Sociable, with a side-seat so a passenger could come along for the ride. There were even a few models with special blades for use on ice.

Ordinary with side-seat attachment   Ordinary on ice

The oddest variations were the giant unicycles. Designers increased the size of the wheel to as much as eight feet and did away with the rest of the frame. The rider sat on a seat suspended from the center axle and moved the wheel with either

Giant wheel unicycle   One-wheeled vehicle

hand or foot pedals. Unfortunately, none of the giant unicycle builders ever figured out a good way to keep the machines balanced while in motion. Happily, a few people made small-wheeled unicycles like this one being ridden by Louis Schutte in 1899.

A postman making his rounds

An ordinary-powered sewing machine

Unicycles never became a popular way to travel, but they did find a great deal of use in circus acts.

But it was the ordinary that captured the imaginations of American riders. Soon policemen and postmen were seen covering wider areas on the machines. And stores discovered that the high-wheeler could be used to deliver small packages. Ordinaries were also used to pump water from wells, to drain flooded fields, and, as this illustration shows, to turn a sewing machine.

The ordinary changed the shape of the bicycle. And it changed the way people traveled and carried out their work. But the biggest change was in who used the ordinary. Not only did men ride ordinaries, but women did, too.

A small number of women rode in bicycle races and were able

Annie Sylvester and her ordinary

to make money at it. Most women riders worked for circuses or fairs and did tricks while circling an arena. Here Annie Sylvester stands beside her bicycle. She dazzled audiences all over America by riding while sitting backward, while standing on the seat—or while balancing on her head. Not many women rode the highwheeler, but those that did opened the way for female bicycle riders of the future.

The ordinary was the first bicycle that was light enough to allow long-distance travel. It could be ridden by men and women and children. And it could even be used for certain types of work. The ordinary put America and the rest of the world on wheels.

4 The Tricycle

During the 1870s and '80s, the ordinary was the most popular kind of bicycle. However, less daring people wanted a safer way to travel. For them manufacturers began making tricycles.

This 1885 family snapshot shows a variety of tricycles. The little boy is on the simplest model. Its pedals are attached to the front wheel, as is the steering handle. The only thing the rear wheels did was hold the machine up. The boy's tricycle doesn't even have a brake. To stop, he had to drag his feet along the ground.

A tricycle family

The mother's tricycle has several improvements over her son's. The large rear wheels were not just for balance, but were also used to power the machine. The front pedals are connected to the rear axle by a chain. When the pedals were turned, the chain made the rear wheels go around. Her machine also has a brake system. When the right handle was turned, a wire made the brake pad rub against the front wheel.

The father and daughter are on the most complicated machines. Their models are similar to this Gromully and Jeffery Ideal Tricycle. The pedals are connected to each other. As they turned, a chain made the rear wheels turn.

While moving, the rider held onto levers on either side of the seat. The lever above the chain operated a brake. When this lever was pushed forward, it rubbed against a metal disc and slowed the machine. The other lever was used for steering. This lever is connected to the front wheel by a long, metal rod. Pushing the lever forward turned the wheel to the left. Pulling back on the lever turned the wheel to the right.

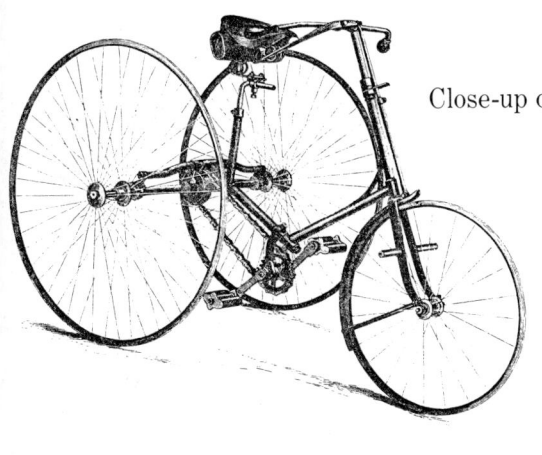

Close-up of the mother's tricycle

The Gromully and Jeffery Ideal Tricycle

Tricycles often weighed over 150 pounds, so they were much slower than the ordinary. But they had important advantages, too. The rider didn't have to have a good sense of balance. And the rider could stop the machine without having to jump down from a high seat. All a rider had to do was sit on a seat, pedal, and not run into anything.

What's more, a tricycle could carry heavy and bulky loads. The rider of an ordinary could carry a light package strapped to his back. On the other hand, the wicker basket of this 1890 Peugeot Tricycle Porteur held over 110 pounds of goods. This made a tricycle particularly valuable to businesses.

Tricycle with package carrier

Tricycles could also be built so that two people could sit side by side. Here a couple are happily gliding down New York's Riverside Drive on a summer night in 1886. The two-seater meant that riders could chat while moving. It also meant that there would be two pair of legs for pedaling up steep hills.

It wasn't long before designers began fitting tricycles with steam engines. Lucius D. Copeland was one of the first to do this in 1887.

A ride along Riverside Drive

The Copeland steam tricycle

Copeland was able to build a small, light steam engine. It was quieter and more reliable than the one Sylvester Roper had built twenty years before. And it was powerful enough to move the tricycle, the driver, and a passenger.

Copeland's machine was so successful that bicycle manufacturers around the world copied the idea. This 1891 photo shows workers assembling motorized tricycles for Peugeot. By the end of the century, several bicycle makers were not only selling bicycles, tricycles, and unicycles, but motorcycles, motorized tricycles, and four-wheeled contraptions that came to be called automobiles.

Tricycle factory

5 From Safety to Modern Racer

Riders all over the world seemed happy with the ordinary and the tricycle. The roads were full of these machines and more were appearing every day. But designers kept tinkering with the shape and size of the bicycle. They were trying to come up with a design that everyone could ride.

In 1879, an Englishman named H. J. Lawson devloped the Bicyclette. It looked a little like an old boneshaker. And as with the boneshaker, the rider sat between the two wheels a little above the metal frame. The difference was in how the wheels were turned. The front-wheel pedals were gone. Instead, the rear wheel was turned by a pedal-chain system.

People thought the Bicyclette was ugly, so not many of them were ever made. But other designers liked Lawson's idea. The most successful adaptation of the Lawson Bicyclette was made in 1885 by James Starley's nephew, John Kemp Starley. Starley called his machine the Rover. This 1889 St. George's New Rapid Bicycle was very similar to the Starley Rover.

A bicycle of this shape had a number of advantages over the ordinary and tricycle. It was lighter. Most weighed thirty pounds

The St. George's New Rapid Bicycle

or less. This made it particularly handy for people who lived in the city. A rider could easily carry one up the winding stairs and store it in a hallway.

The small wheels allowed a rider to get on and off without much trouble. And because the rider sat well behind the front wheel, there was no chance of a "header," even if the brakes were jammed on. The design was so safe that any bicycle built like this came to be called a "safety."

The safety bicycle became popular with women instantly. By using a drop-frame, a woman could ride a safety even while wearing a long dress. The illustration of this drop-frame bicycle shows two other improvements. A chain guard was added to prevent the rider's dress from getting snagged in the chain. Front and rear fenders stopped mud from splattering on the rider.

Bicycling on Fifth Avenue

Drop-frame bicycle with chain guard and fenders

At first, men were reluctant to give up the ordinary. The large wheels of the ordinary made it faster than most of the early safety bicycles. Also, many men actually liked the danger involved in riding an ordinary. They felt it required a special skill and daring, similar to that shown by cavalry soldiers. Two improvements to the safety eventually won these men over.

The first was the invention of the air-filled, or pneumatic, tire. This was developed in 1885 by a Scottish veterinarian named John Boyd Dunlop.

When pneumatic tires first appeared many people criticized them. The rough roads often made the tires lose air. And occasionally a tire would slip off the rim and cause an accident. Once Dunlop had solved these problems, riders discovered that air-filled tires softened the bumpy ride better than the solid rubber ones. More important, they were much lighter than the old-fashioned tires and this increased the speed of the safety.

The second improvement happened in 1898. Up until this time, the pedals of all bicycles and tricycles continued to turn as long as the machine was moving. If a rider wanted to rest his legs, he had to dangle them to the side or put them on a footrest. The introduction of the coaster-brake changed this.

The coaster-brake allowed a rider to "freewheel." The wheels of the bicycle continued to turn, but the pedals didn't. That meant that the rider could keep his feet on the pedals at all times.

The coaster-brake also made stopping easier. The rider simply rotated the pedals backwards. This made a cone-shaped piece of metal rub against the inside of the rear wheel. Coaster-brakes worked so well that they could instantly stop a wheel from turning.

A few riders put pneumatic tires on their ordinaries. This cushioned the ride a little, but didn't add much speed. But putting coaster-brakes on an ordinary wasn't very practical. Coaster-brakes could stop a high-wheeler quickly, but every time a rider did this, he had to hop down from the seat before he fell over. Soon safety bicycles designed for racing were beating ordinaries handily—and men began trading in their high-wheelers. In 1889, there were around 200,000 safeties in the United States. Ten years later, there were over 1,250,000 of them on the road.

Men and women were pedaling to work on their safeties. They used them to go to the market, to travel to the country for a picnic, or just to get to a neighbor's house. The safety was so simple to use that even young children were able to ride full-sized machines. The famous photographer Jacob Riis caught this Western Union messenger just as he was leaving to deliver a telegram.

Not only was the safety easy to ride, but the basic design could be altered without much trouble. The best known variation is the tandem.

Night messenger for Western Union

At first, the two-seater was only a regular safety with an extra seat. This 1890 Peugeot Tandem Bicyclette has a second seat attached above the rear wheel. The second rider had a set of pedals and a handbrake, too. In addition, the rear handlebar is connected to the front one by a steel bar. When a turn was going to be made, one of the riders had to call out "right" or "left" to be sure they both turned in the same direction.

This seat arrangement didn't give the second rider much legroom, and the position was awkward for pedaling. Designers solved the problem by making the frame longer. This can be seen clearly in the Columbia tandem, which Mr. and Mrs. Goldsmith rode throughout France in 1889.

The Goldsmiths in France

Designers were concerned that the longer frame might not support the weight of two adults. To insure an unbending frame, additional tubing was added to the frame. Surprisingly, tandems were still fairly light. The Goldsmith's machine weighed only forty-six pounds, which was less than the weight of most ordinaries.

The success of the tandem led designers to have even bigger ideas. Peugeot not only offered a tandem, but a three- and four-seater as well. Note the extra support bar that runs the entire length of the Quadruplette.

[40]

Safety tandem

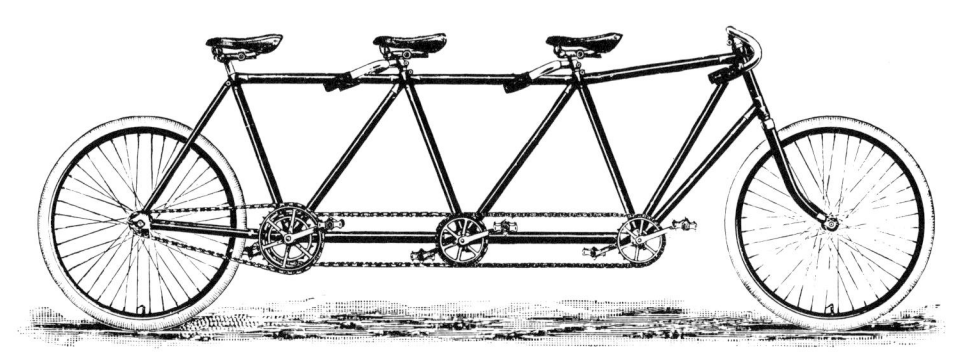

The Triplette

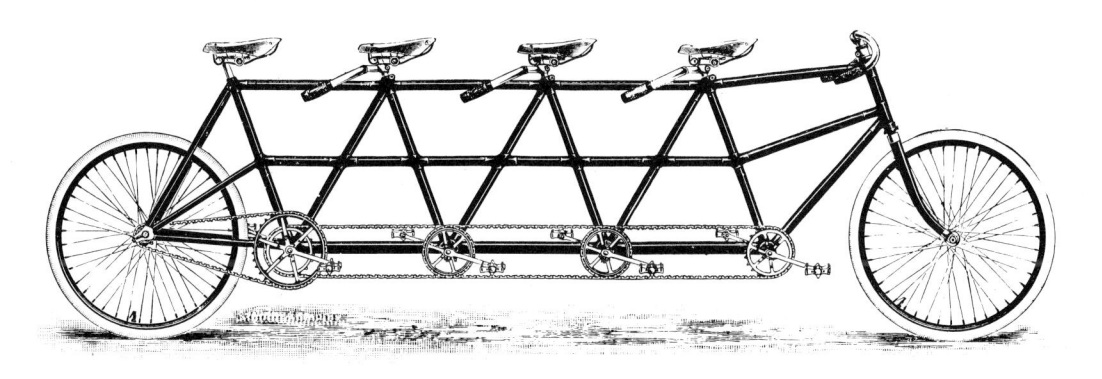

The Quadruplette

Safety bicycles with rail attachments

Other design variations were more unusual. This group of cyclists is out for a carefree ride along a little-used section of the Pittsburgh and Western Railroad. The rail attachements had two purposes. First, they kept the bicycle perfectly centered on the thin rail. Second, they kept the bicycle and rider in an upright position. Without having to concentrate on balancing, the rider could enjoy the passing scenery—and listen for oncoming trains. An added feature is the wooden platform on the lead safety. It provided the perfect seat for a child.

Another odd-looking machine was the 1898 Rex Cycle invented by Bohn C. Hicks. Hicks wanted to design a bicycle that would absorb the shocks of a bumpy road.

The seat of the Rex is mounted on a curving, metal bar that is hinged to the main frame. A small third wheel is attached to the back of the bar. As the wheels went over rocks or holes, the seat bar rose and fell gently. This sounds like a good idea, but the extra wheel and metal tubing made the Rex heavy and slow moving. Riders didn't think the ride was smooth enough to justify the additional effort needed to pedal it, so the Rex never became very popular.

If the Rex Cycle was clunky, this 1900 Pierce Bicycle was the ultimate in elegance. Its main feature was that it didn't have a greasy chain. The designer of this machine did away with the chain. Instead he had a driveshaft go from the pedals to the rear wheels. The driveshaft was inside a metal tube. This insured that grease couldn't get on the rider's clothes. Making this bicycle cost a great deal of money and not many Pierce Bicycles were ever seen on the road. Later, the Pierce Company gave up bicycle manufacturing to produce the famous Pierce Arrow automobile.

Forty-four years later, people were still trying to think up new ideas on the original safety design. John Whalen and Webster Janssen fashioned this Laminated-Wood-Frame-Bicycle in 1942. The Second World War was raging in Europe at the time and metal was scarce. But their wooden bicycle was never put into production. Soon after they completed it, wood became even more scarce than metal.

Some of these variations are fun to look at. Others, like the Rex Cycle, might seem very silly to us. The important thing is that these and many other designers were trying to improve the bicycle. They wanted to make it carry more people, or be cleaner or more comfortable to ride. Then an odd thing happened in the history of the bicycle.

The Rex Cycle, 1898

The Pierce

Whalen and Janssen wooden bicycle

Since the introduction of the ordinary, people in the United States had been avid riders. Then between 1910 and 1920 everyone seemed to lose interest in the safety. The reason for this was the automobile.

Inexpensive, mass-produced cars began to appear as early as 1901. By 1915, a few models could go fifty miles per hour with four passengers. The roof and side-flaps protected the riders from rain and snow. And with gasoline costing only pennies a gallon, a car was cheap to run. The question became: why pedal when it's easier and cheaper to ride? In 1908, 63,500 cars were made. Twelve years later, the annual production of cars had risen to over 2,000,000!

Millions of people in the United States still owned bicycles, but they used them less and less. And as bicycle sales dropped, manufacturers lost interest in trying to redesign and improve them. The bicycles that were ridden in 1970 were almost the same as those used in 1900!

In Europe, the situation was much different. Gasoline had to be imported and was always expensive. People depended less on their cars for their everyday transportation. They might use a car for a long trip or to haul heavy loads, but the bicycle still got them to work or the store. As a result, European manufacturers continued to improve the bicycle.

The chief aim was to make the bicycle lighter. There are many mountain ranges throughout Europe, so every ounce of weight makes it a little harder to pedal up steep hills. To help riders climb these hills, designers made the frames and tire rims as thin as possible and gearing systems were developed. Gearing systems were actually first developed around 1864 to get the heavy tricycles up hills. Designers discovered that they could increase speed by changing the size of the rear-wheel hub and the chainwheel. These are the toothed metal discs the chain goes around. The speed increased because with each turn of the pedal the wheels went around more than one time.

An early two-speed bicycle

The same concept was later used on pedal-chain-driven two-wheelers. This 1888 Bicyclette à Deux Vitesses is an example of one of the earliest two-speed bicycles. It's not entirely clear how this gearing system worked, but the catalog did state that "repeated tests done on large ramps have demonstrated positively that with a machine equipped with our system, you can climb slopes inaccessible to the rider mounted on an ordinary machine."

But riders weren't always going uphill. Sometimes they were on flat ground and didn't want to go fast. And the steepness of hills varied. To overcome this problem, front and rear derailleur systems were invented. By changing the lever position, the rider could jump the chain from one size wheel hub and chainwheel to another. The rider could choose the gear he wanted, depending on the size of the hill and how fast he wanted to go. Modern bicycles can have from three to eighteen gears.

Close-up of gear handle   Front derailleur system    Rear derailleur system

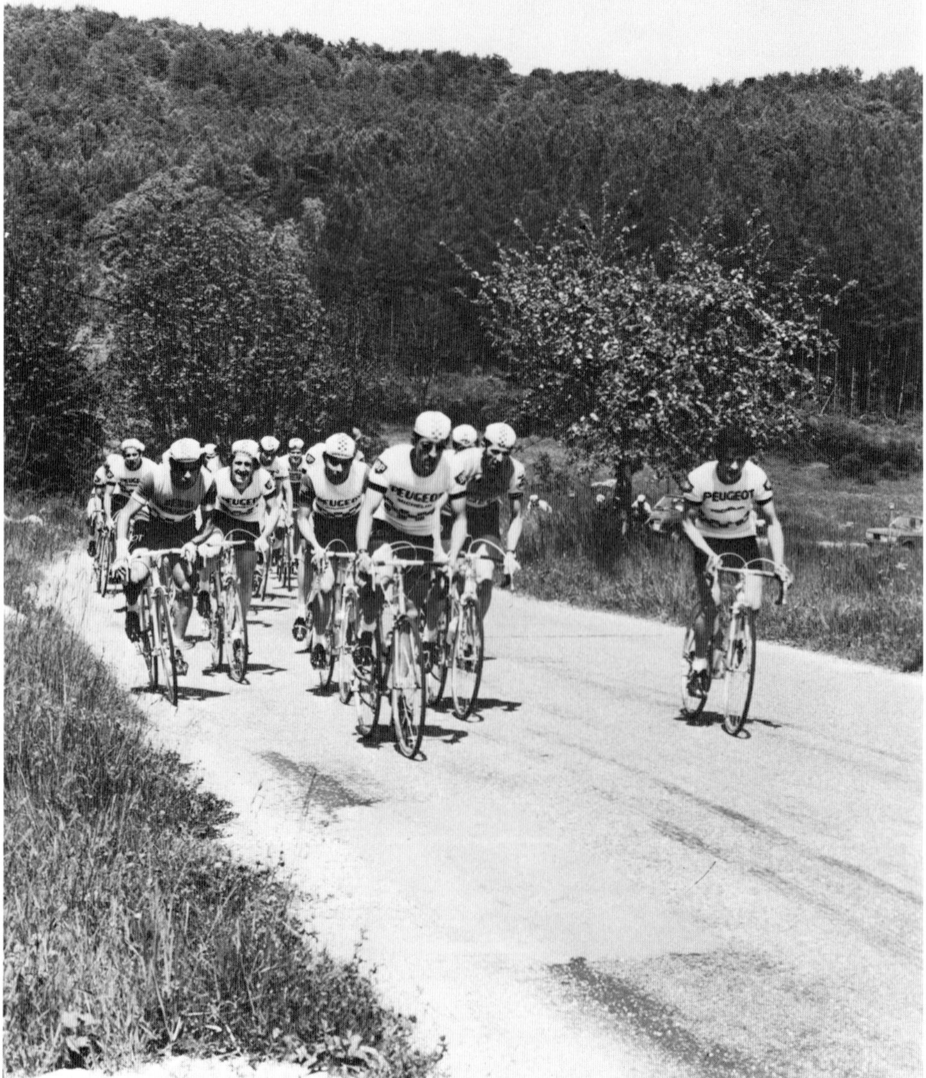
PEUGEOT
PEUGEOT
PEUGEOT
PEUGEOT

Next, European designers improved the braking system. The old type that had a brake shoe rub against the tire didn't always stop the bicycle quickly. Also, the shoe rubbing against the tire made the brake shoe and tire wear out. The coaster-brake stopped the wheel instantly, but often caused the wheel to lock up and skid. Skidding wore out tires quickly. The caliper brake solved the problem.

The caliper brake had two soft rubber pads attached to hinged, metal fingers. When the handle was squeezed, a metal wire pulled the fingers together and the rubber pads touched the smooth metal of the wheel rim. This slowed the wheels without causing either the tires or the brake pads to wear out. By using both front and rear caliper brakes, a rider could stop his machine as quickly as with coaster-brakes.

All these changes created the lightweight, but sturdy, bicycle we're familiar with today.

These bicycles didn't become popular in the United States until early in the 1970s. That was when gas prices began to go up

Left: The Peugeot racing team practices hill climbing

Front brake pads

The Windsor Touring Bicycle

sharply and gas shortages created long lines at the filling stations. People once again discovered that it was much easier—and cheaper—to pedal to work or the store.

At the same time as this was happening many Americans became concerned with their physical fitness. Millions of people took to the bicycle for exercise. A few preferred to stay indoors. But many more simply packed their bags and took to the road.

Today, bicycle makers offer a wide variety of machines for every need. There are bicycles for road racing or long-distance touring or just for a leisurely ride down the street. Unicycles, tandems, and exercise machines are available. There are even specially designed BMX racers with tires that grip the sharp turns and frames strong enough to withstand the impact of a high jump. The kind of bicycle you ride depends on how far you want to go, what you intend to carry, and how fast you want to get there.

Exercising on an indoor cycle

A BMX racer sails over a bump

Modern bicycles fitted with touring packs

[51]

6 Human-Powered Vehicles

The driver climbs into his bullet-shaped Vector at 8:30 A.M. and pulls the canopy shut. A minute later he is cruising down the interstate highway on the way to work.

A quick check of the instrument panel tells him he is doing just over sixty miles per hour. The panel also lets the driver know his temperature, heartbeat, and the number of calories he is burning up. Everything seems normal as he passes a line of slow-moving cars and buses and turns up a ramp marked: "HPVs Only."

As he pulls into his parking space, the driver notes that the trip took twenty minutes—much faster than when he drove his old Datsun. What's more, he didn't use any gasoline. He'd made the trip by using simple pedal-power.

This might sound like a scene from the distant future, but it's not. The Vector has already been built. And there are a lot of

The vector

[52]

Sitting upright allows wind to hit more of the body

A racing crouch reduces area hit

other human-powered vehicles being tested that could replace the present day bicycle.

The biggest problem with modern bicycles is wind drag. When a rider is going forward, he is moving through air. The air hits the rider in the chest, head, legs, and arms and slows him down. The air also hits the bicycle. At twenty miles per hour, a rider has to use half of his energy just to get through the air. The only way to overcome wind drag is by streamlining the rider and bicycle.

One way to do this is to have the rider crouch over while in motion. This doesn't eliminate wind drag completely, but by having a smaller area hit by the air, it does reduce it. Another way to streamline is to have the rider wear skintight clothing. This allows the air to flow around the rider's body.

[53]

The most efficient way to reduce wind drag is to streamline the entire bicycle.

Streamlining isn't a new idea. In 1915, E. Bunai Varilla was granted a patent for a "wind-easing apparatus." Varilla attached a shell, or fairing, to a safety bicycle. His fairing was made of thin pieces of wood with canvas glued to the outside. It must have looked like a giant, bulging envelope with wheels, but it did cut through the air with its pointy front.

Two Frenchmen put Varilla's concept to work. Marcel Berthet rode his Velodyne to a world record speed of 30 miles per hour in 1933. A few years later, Francois Faure set a new record of 31.40 miles per hour in his Velocar. Unfortunately, neither record was allowed to stand. The International Cycling Federation ruled that only standard-shaped bicycles would be allowed to compete in races or to set speed records.

The idea of streamlining might have been forgotten forever if it weren't for the International Human-Powered Vehicle Association, which was formed in 1975. The IHPVA is a group of designers and engineers who want to improve the performance of any shaped wheeled machine. The only rule is that the vehicle be powered by humans and not by any sort of engine.

Some of the designs that resulted from the IHPVA's annual competitions might have seemed very familiar to Varilla.

Most modern variations are very different looking. Some rode their two-wheeled bicycles while lying on their stomachs. This position reduced the area of their bodies hit directly by air. The only problem with this idea is that someone has to hold the rider upright before he can get his vehicle in motion—and someone has to catch him whenever he wants to stop.

Other designs ride low to the ground. The Vector is the best example of this kind of machine. The Vector was designed by a group of California engineers—Al Voight, Dan Fernandes, John Speicher, and Doug Unkrey. They took a lightweight, three-wheeled frame and put a sleek, fiber glass shell over it. A clear plastic canopy lets the driver see in all directions.

Inside, the driver sits low to the ground with the pedals at the front of the machine. A simple rudder stick is used for steering and also has a handle for the brakes and a six-speed gearshift lever. A speedometer and mini-computer are also mounted inside the vehicle.

Amazingly, this complicated machine weighs only 51 pounds. And because it is so streamlined and easy to pedal, it has already been driven at a world record 58 miles per hour. The Vector designers believe that with a few changes their machine can top 100 miles per hour!

So far, all HPVs are made by hand and ridden only on test tracks. But a few bicycle manufacturers hope to have their first HPVs ready for sale by 1985. In ten years, the sleek racing bicycles of today might be considered as old-fashioned as the safety or as odd-looking as the ordinary. And when you want to go somewhere, you'll hop into a Vector and glide silently along the street without much effort.

A group on a cross-country tour

Anatomy of a Bicycle

The modern multi-speed bicycle came about through 200 years of slow change and experimentation. The Comte de Sivrac's celerifere had two wheels with spokes, a simple wooden frame, and a handle. Modern bicycles are made of a great many parts. This chart shows the names and locations of the major parts of a Peugeot ten-speed touring bicycle.

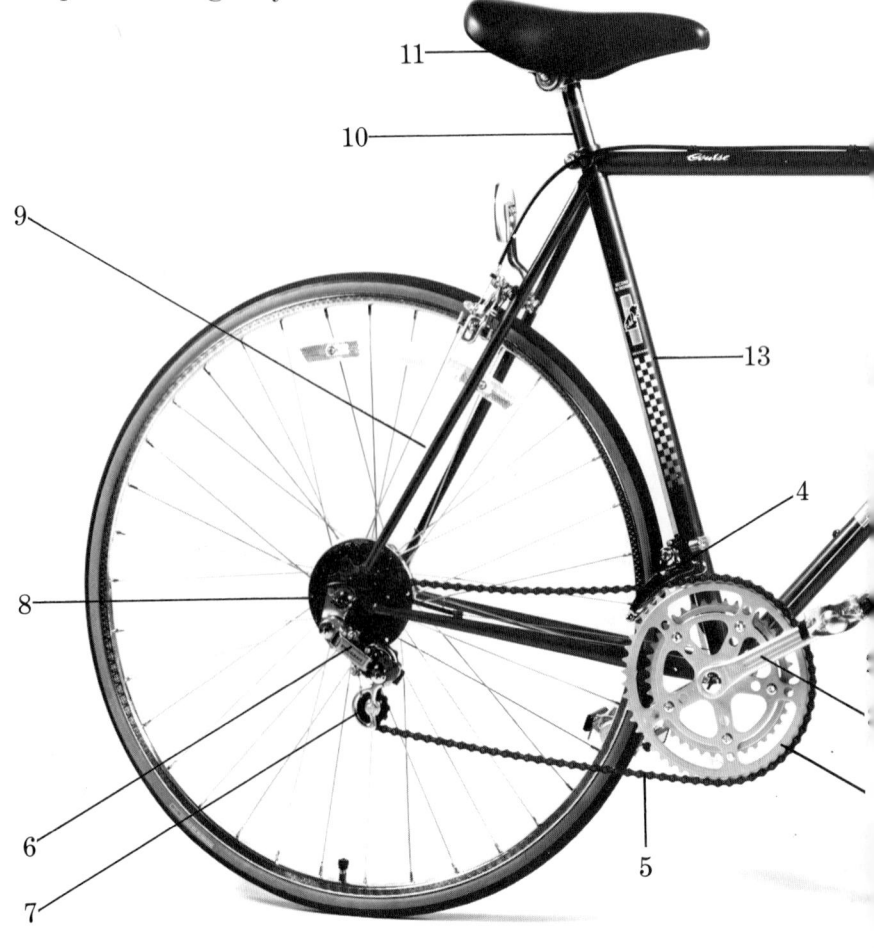

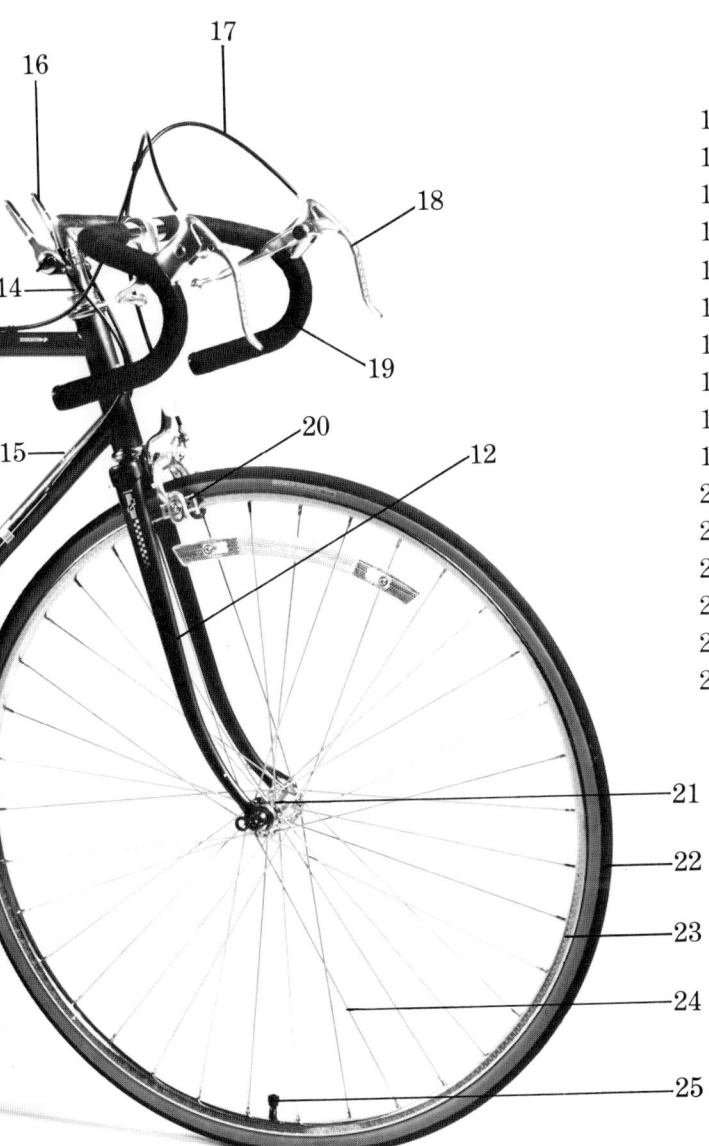

1. Chainwheel
2. Pedal
3. Crank
4. Front derailleur
5. Chain
6. Rear derailleur
7. Derailleur tension roller
8. Freewheel gear cluster
9. Seat stay
10. Seat post
11. Saddle (or seat)
12. Fork
13. Seat mast
14. Handlebar stem
15. Bottom tube (or down tube)
16. Gearshift lever
17. Brake cable
18. Brake lever
19. Handlebars
20. Caliper brake
21. Hub
22. Tire
23. Rim
24. Spoke
25. Valve

For Further Reading

Alderson, Frederick. *Bicycling: A History.* New York: Praeger Publishing Co., 1972.

Boethling, Bob, ed. *The Bicycle Book.* Los Angeles: UCLA Alumni Association, 1971.

Burstyn, Ben. *Bicycle Repair and Maintenance.* New York: Arco Publishing Co., 1974.

Coles, Clarence. *Glenn's Complete Bicycle Manual.* New York: Crown Publishers, 1973.

Colligan, Douglas. *The Cyclist's Manual.* New York: Sterling Publishing Co., 1981.

De la Rosa, Denise M. *Understanding, Maintaining and Riding the Ten-Speed Bicycle.* Emmaus, Penn.: Rodale Books, 1979.

Gorey, Edward. *The Broken Spoke.* New York: Dodd, Mead & Co., 1976.

McCullagh, James, ed. *American Bicycle Racing.* Emmaus, Penn.: Rodale Books, 1976.

Oliver, Smith Hempstone and Berkebile, Donald H. *Wheels and Wheeling: The Smithsonian Cycle Collection.* Washington, D.C.: Smithsonian Institution Press, 1974.

Saroyan, William. *The Bicycle Rider in Beverly Hills.* New York: Charles Scribner's and Sons, 1952.

Smith, Robert A. *A Social History of the Bicycle.* New York: American Heritage Press, 1972.

Wilcockson, John. *Bicycle.* New York: Butterick Publishers, 1980.

Wilhelm, Tim. *The Bicycle Touring Book.* Emmaus, Penn.: Rodale Books, 1980.

Index

Page entries in *italics* refer to illustrations.

Ariel, 19
automobiles, 35, 46

Berthet, Marcel, 54
bicycles
   anatomy of, 56-57, *56-57*
   invention of, 1
Bicyclette, 35
Bicyclette à Deux Vitesses, 47
blades, 26, *26*
BMX racers, 50, *51*
boneshakers, 10-14, *10*, *11*, *12*, 18
   schools, 13, *13*
   tandems, 14, *14*
Boston Bicycle Club, 19, *20-21*
brake shoes, 12-13
braking system, 49, *49*

caliper brake, 49
celeriferes, 3-4, *3*
coaster-brake, 38, 49
Columbia ordinary, *18*
Columbia tandem, 40
Copeland, Lucius D., 32-34
Copeland steam tricycle, 32, *33*

Dandy Horse, 5
Datsun, 52
derailleur system, 47, *47*
Drais, Baron Karl von, 4-7
Draisienne, 5, *5*
Drais rudder, 11
drop-frame bicycle, 36, *37*
Dunlop, John Boyd, 38

Egyptians, bicyclelike machines of, 1
exercise machines, 50, *51*

Fat Man's Cycle Club, 22
Faure, Francois, 54
Fernandes, Dan, 54
four-seaters, 40-41

gasoline engines, 15
gearing system, 46-47, *47*
Germantown Bicycle Club, 17, *17*
Goldsmith, Mr. and Mrs., 40, *40*
Gompertz, Lewis, 9
Gompertz velocipede, 9, *9*
Gromully and Jeffery Ideal Tricycle, 31, *31*

handlebars, 11
"header," 19, 26, 36
Hedstrom, Oscar, 15
Hicks, Bohn C., 44
high-wheelers, 17-19
Honda XR500R, 16, *16*
horses
   hobbyhorses vs., 4, *4*
   wheeled, 2, 3
human-powered vehicles, 52-55

Indian Motorcycle, 15, *16*
International Cycling Federation, 54
International Human-Powered Vehicle
   Association (IHPVA), 54

Janssen, Webster, 44
Johnson's Pedestrian Hobby Horse School, 7, *7*

Ladies' Hobby Horse, 8-9, *8*
Lallement, Pierre, 11
Laminated-Wood-Frame-Bicycle, 44, *45*

[59]

Lawson, H. J., 35
League of American Wheelmen, 22
Leonardo da Vinci, tricycle of, 1-2, *1*
Louis XVI, King of France, 3-4

mail, delivery of, 9, 28
Michaux, Pierre, 10-11, 14
motorcycles, 16, 34
motors, on bicycles, 15

one-wheeled vehicle, *27*
ordinaries, 17-29
    with blades, 26, *26*
    for children, 26
    with side-seat attachment, 26, *26*
    with small front wheels, 25-26, *26*

package carrier, 32, *32*
pedal-chain system, 35
pedals, 10, 12
Pedestrian Hobby Horse, 5
Peugeot Tandem Bicyclette, 40
Peugeot ten-speed, 56, *56-57*
Peugeot Tricycle Porteur, 32
Pierce Arrow automobile, 44
Pierce Bicycle, 44, *45*
Pitman, Will, 22
policemen, 28
postmen, 9, *27*, 28
pumps, ordinary-powered, 28

Quadruplette, 40, *41*

races, 22-25, *24*, *25*, *48*
    attire for, 22, 53
    spotters for, 25
rail attachments, 42-43, *42-43*
Rex Cycle, 44, *45*
Riis, Jacob, 39
Rising Sun Cycle Club, 22
Roper, Sylvester, 14, 16, 34
Roper steam velocipede, 14-15, *15*
Rover, 35

safety bicycles, 36-51, *41*
    with rail attachment, 42-43, *42-43*
St. George's New Rapid Bicycle, *36*

Schutte, Louis, 27
sewing machines, 28, *28*
side-seat attachments, 26, *26*
Sivrac, Comte de, 3, 56
Sociable, 26
Speicher, John, 54
Starley, James, 19, 35
Starley, John Kemp, 35
steam engines, 14, 32, *33*
Stokes Poges two-wheeler, 2, *2*
Swiftwalker, 5
Sylvester, Annie, 29, *29*

tandems, 14, *14*, 39-41, *41*, 50
telegrams, delivery of, 39, *39*
three-seaters, 40-41
tires
    air-filled, 38
    rubber vs. iron, 18
tricycles, 30-34, *30*, *31*, *33*
    of da Vinci, 1-2, *1*
    factory, *34*
    with package carrier, 32, *32*
    steam engine and, 32, *32*, 34
Triplette, *41*
two-seaters, 14, 32, 40
two-speed bicycles, 47, *47*

unicycles
    giant-wheeled, 27, *27*
    small-wheeled, 27
Unkrey, Doug, 54

Varilla, E. Bunai, 54
Vector, 52, *52*, 54-55
    mini-computer in, 55
Velocipedes, 5-14, *6*
Velodyne, 54
Voight, Al, 54

Whalen, John, 44
wheelies, world's first, 4
Windsor Touring Bicycle, *50*
women riders, 7-9, 28-29, 36
wooden bicycles, 44, *45*
Wright, M. W., 22-23
    racer of, *23*